W9-BGW-488

WITHDRAWN

JUN 15 1998

RIVER
AND
STREAM

APRIL PULLEY SAYRE

TWENTY-FIRST CENTURY BOOKS

A Division of Henry Holt and Company
• New York •

*For Chris and Becky, in thanks for their encouragement,
their air-conditioning, and their wave pool.*

ACKNOWLEDGMENTS

Our thanks to Dr. John Waldman of the Hudson River
Foundation, and Dr. Gary Lamberti of Notre Dame University,
who reviewed portions of this text.

Twenty-First Century Books
A Division of Henry Holt and Company, Inc.
115 West 18th Street
New York, NY 10011

Henry Holt® and colophon are trademarks of
Henry Holt and Company, Inc.
Publishers since 1866

Text copyright © 1996 by April Pulley Sayre
Illustrations © 1996 by Martha Weston
All rights reserved.
Published in Canada by Fitzhenry & Whiteside Ltd.
195 Allstate Parkway, Markham, Ontario L3R 4T8

Library of Congress Cataloging-in-Publication Data
Sayre, April Pulley.
River and Stream / April Pulley Sayre. — 1st ed.
p. cm. — (Exploring earth's biomes)
Includes index.
Summary: Describes aquatic biomes, focusing on life in rivers
and streams, and explains the effect of pollution on these
biotic communities and on the lives of people everywhere.
1. Stream ecology—Juvenile literature. 2. Rivers—Juvenile literature.
3. Stream ecology—North America—Juvenile literature. 4. Rivers—North
America—Juvenile literature. [1. Stream ecology. 2. Rivers. 3. Ecology.]
I. Title. II. Series: Sayre, April Pulley.
Exploring earth's biomes.
QH541.5.S7S28 1996   574.5'26323'097—dc20
95–34458   CIP
                                                             AC

ISBN 0–8050–4088–9
First Edition—1996

Cover design by Betty Lew
Interior design by Kelly Soong

Printed in the United States of America
All first editions are printed on acid-free paper ∞.
10 9 8 7 6 5 4 3 2 1

Photo credits appear on page 80.

CONTENTS

INTRODUCTION TO AQUATIC BIOMES

The water that makes up more than two-thirds of your body weight, that flows in your blood, that bathes your cells, and that you cry as tears, may once have flowed in a river. It may have floated as a cloud, fallen as a snowflake, bobbed in ocean waves, or been drunk by a dinosaur from an ancient lake. All this is possible because the water that's presently on earth has always been here—except for ice brought by comets hitting the earth's atmosphere. And all the water on earth is connected in a global cycle. This cycle is called the water cycle, or the hydrologic cycle.

Every day, all over the earth, water exists in and moves through this cycle. Ninety-seven percent of the earth's water is in the oceans. Two percent is in frozen glaciers and ice caps at the Poles. The remaining 1 percent is divided among the world's lakes, rivers, groundwater, soil moisture, and water vapor in the air. All this comes to a grand total of 326 million cubic miles (1,359 million cubic kilometers) of water. Every day, this water is exchanged among the oceans, streams, clouds, glaciers, lakes, wetlands, and even dew-covered leaves. Even now, it is being exhaled from your body, as moisture in your breath.

As the water cycles, at times it changes phase from solid to liquid to gas. The heat of the sun warms water on the land's surface, in lakes, in streams, in the ocean, even on the leaves of plants—and causes this water to evaporate, to turn into a gas. This gas rises into the air, cools, and condenses, eventually forming clouds and falling back to earth as liquid rain or solid snow or hail. This precipitation makes its way into streams, rivers, lakes, oceans, glaciers, and ice caps, and underground. And so the cycle continues. But it's not quite so simple. Each portion of the cycle is connected to others. For example, river water runs into oceans, stream water runs into lakes, and water from underground bubbles out of springs and into rivers. Water is constantly being exchanged among all the many places it resides on planet earth.

Almost anywhere water exists as a liquid, it is colonized by organisms—bacteria, amoebas, fungi, animals, or plants. Some watery habitats have particular physical conditions and particular kinds of plants and animals inhabiting them. These are aquatic biomes: ocean, river, lake, and coral reef. Where these aquatic biomes mingle with terrestrial, or land, biomes, they may form special, semiaquatic, fringe communities. Wetland and seashore are two of these communities that are unique enough and widespread enough to qualify as major biomes.

All aquatic and semiaquatic biomes—ocean, river, lake, coral reef, seashore, and wetland—are influenced by regional climate and the lands nearby. These biomes are also linked to one another, by ever-moving water molecules and the global water cycle through which they flow.

ᔑ 1 ᔐ
THE RIVER AND STREAM BIOME

Draining 1,000 streams and carrying one-fifth of the world's river water, the Amazon is the giant of all rivers. It's so big and so ancient that it contains 1,300 species of fish, more than the entire Atlantic Ocean. Yet the world's other rivers have remarkable physical and biological features, too. The Ganges River, considered sacred by Hindu people, arises from snowfields and ice caves high in the Himalayas. Venezuela's Angel Falls, the world's highest waterfall, cascades down 3,213 feet (979 meters). The Mississippi River has dumped billions of tons of silt, forming the land on which New Orleans sits. And other rivers harbor extraordinary aquatic animals: the Zaire River—a strange upside-down catfish, the Nile River—enormous hippos, the Yangtze River—playful river dolphins, and Australian rivers—oddball creatures called duck-billed platypuses.

Unlike lake waters, river waters are constantly flowing. They are dynamic habitats: a desert river can swell from a trickle to a 10-foot- (3-meter-) deep flood in just a few hours. A quiet, slow-moving stream can become a curtain of fast-flowing water as it hurtles over a waterfall's lip. Even when a river meets the sea, it may still flow on for a time, scouring a deep ravine on the ocean floor.

A river's or stream's current shapes the lives of animals and plants within it. Mosses have holdfast roots that anchor

7

The setting sun glistens on the Mississippi River.

them to the riverbed. Natural hooks, anchors, lines, and suction cups help aquatic insects cling to rocks. Crayfish find shelter beneath stones, only scurrying out to snatch tidbits of food that pass by.

While many people use the term *stream* for a small body of water and the term *river* for a larger one, the two terms are used by most scientists interchangeably. After all, rivers and streams are part of the same interconnected system. As a whole, the system is considered a biome—an area that has a certain kind of community of plants and animals living in it. A river system is aquatic—a water biome. And it's a freshwater biome, meaning its water is not salty as in the ocean—a marine biome.

Unlike terrestrial biomes, such as grassland, desert, and tundra, the river and stream biome does not have a characteristic climate. It is strongly affected by the terrestrial biomes through which it flows. Outside influences—not just climate but tree leaves that fall into the water, land animals that visit its waters, and rainwater running off the land—all influence the river and its inhabitants. River and land also intermingle to form riparian habitat: a unique streamside zone full of birds, frogs, turtles, trees, wildflowers, and other organisms.

8

TYPES
There are three main types of rivers:
- Permanent streams, which flow year-round and are by far the most common.
- Intermittent streams, which flow only during certain seasons, after storms or when snow melts in spring.
- Interrupted streams, which flow aboveground in some places and below ground in others.

DIVISIONS
Rivers are classified according to their channel shape. There may be several types of channels along the length of a single river. The main shapes are:
- Straight streams, which run in a fairly uncurving line.
- Meandering streams, which loop and curve.
- Braided streams, which consist of several streams of water, intermingling and braiding, and separated by sand and gravel bars.

PHYSICAL FEATURES
Rivers generally have the following features:
- A one-way flow of water (except in estuaries, where water may flow upriver on the rising tide).
- Fresh water (except in estuaries, where the river's fresh water mixes with salty ocean water).
- A downhill course, from areas of high altitude to low altitude.
- More water at their end than at their start.
- A tendency to erode, transport, and deposit sediment.
- An ability to shape the land, creating landforms such as deltas, canyons, and gorges.

ANIMALS

- Insect larvae commonly have hooks, suckers, a flattened shape, and other adaptations to stay in place in fast-moving streams.
- Rivers and streams have a greater number of species than is found in lakes.
- Many animals from surrounding areas depend on streams for food and water.
- Worms, insect larvae, fish, and crustaceans are common.

PLANTS

- Plants, especially in fast-moving streams, are adapted to withstand water flow.
- Algae, mosses, and liverworts are common.
- Rivers and streams are bordered by important zones called riparian habitat.

❧ 2 ❧
NORTH AMERICAN
RIVERS AND STREAMS

In North America's oldest mountains, the Ozarks, clear-water rivers gush out of springs, plunge through deep ravines, and pour into underground limestone caverns. In the mountains of Nevada, the Humboldt River follows a winding course before drying up in the desert, among the sagebrush, coyotes, and mudflats. And in Tennessee, the force of the Tennessee River flowing over a dam creates the electricity that keeps Knoxville alight.

North America is home to some of the greatest rivers on earth. The Mississippi is among the longest. Canada's Saint Lawrence River has one of the largest discharges, because it drains the Great Lakes. The Colorado River's flow carved the Grand Canyon, which is 217 miles (350 kilometers) long, 18 miles (29 kilometers) across at its widest, and a mile deep in places.

Every brook, stream, or river drains an area of land called its watershed. North America has several major watersheds, also called drainage basins. Most of the water between the Appalachian Mountains and the Rockies flows into the Mississippi-Missouri River system and flows out through Louisiana into the Gulf of Mexico. Water from the Great Lakes, which are all connected, flows eastward out the Saint Lawrence River into the Atlantic Ocean. To the east of the Appalachians, several relatively small rivers also

11

Atlantic Ocean

Gulf of Mexico

Pacific Ocean

St. Lawrence River

Hudson River

APPALACHIAN MOUNTAINS

Lake Ontario

Lake Huron

Lake Superior

Lake Erie

Lake Michigan

Ohio River

Tennessee River

Mississippi River

Missouri River

Arkansas River

ROCKY MOUNTAINS

SIERRA MADRE

CONTINENTAL DIVIDE

Colorado River

CASCADE RANGE

Snake River

SIERRA NEVADA

Columbia River

Sacramento River

San Joaquin River

carry water to the Atlantic Ocean. To the west of the Cascades, Rockies, and Sierra Madre, two major rivers drain the land. The Columbia River carries water to the Pacific Ocean. The Colorado River drains the southwest United States.

Because of these watersheds, at the crest of a mountain, two raindrops, one on each side of the peak, can drain into two different rivers and, eventually, even into two different oceans. The Continental Divide, which runs roughly north to south through the Rocky Mountains, is the border between areas of land that drain westward into the Pacific Ocean and those that drain eastward into the Mississippi River or out the Saint Lawrence River to the Atlantic. Two raindrops falling close together but on opposite sides of the Continental Divide would indeed flow into different oceans.

North America's rivers run through a variety of habitats, including forest, desert, grassland, taiga, and tundra. From clear, fast-running mountain streams to lazy, muddy bayous, the continent has an amazing variety of streams and rivers. Here are just a few facts about these rivers:

- The Grand Canyon is the remarkable work of the Colorado River. The land has been uplifted by geologic forces over a billion years. At the same time, the river has cut downward into rock, creating the Grand Canyon. The fossils in layer upon layer of exposed canyon walls serve as a record of North America's life through the ages.
- The Snake River "slithers" through 1,038 miles (1,660 kilometers) of rugged land before it meets the Columbia River. The waters of the Snake and its tributaries pass through the Rocky Mountains, the Grand Tetons, Hell's Canyon, and Shoshone Falls before emptying into the Columbia River.

- The Salmon River of Idaho is called the "river of no return" for good reason. Travel by kayak or raft along parts of this river is a wild ride through remote canyons and rapids lined by steep granite walls. But this river's rapids only rate Class I-III in difficulty. For even more of a challenge, try rafting California's Salmon River, which has Class V rapids, the toughest rating.
- The Yukon River, the fifth largest river in the United States, flows through Canada and Alaska. This cold river was the site of mining camps during gold rush days and was featured in many books by the famous author Jack London.
- The Columbia River is known for its salmon, which spend several years in the sea, traveling as far as Japan's coastal waters, before returning to their home river to lay their eggs.
- The Rio Grande, a desert river, starts out in the San Juan Mountains of Colorado, then flows through New Mexico before it turns to form the border between Mexico and Texas. At times the Rio Grande is a muddy, swollen river, at times barely a trickle. Its lower reaches eventually empty into the Gulf of Mexico. Along the way, the Rio Grande flows through Big Bend National Park, a wilderness home to roadrunners, vultures, javelinas, mountain lions, and rare birds.
- During March, in early morning, you can stand on a bridge overlooking the Platte River in Kansas and be almost deafened by the noise. Two hundred thousand sandhill cranes—red crowned, 4-foot- (1.2-meter-) tall birds—stop here to rest and feed during their migration north to Canada and Alaska. Although spring floods can make it into a raging torrent, the Platte often spreads out, inspiring the nickname "the river that's a mile wide and an inch deep."

*Many sandhill cranes stop over in the
Platte River area during their annual migration.*

- The Mississippi River drains streams flowing from West Virginia, to Montana, to Manitoba—a grand total of 41 percent of the continental United States. The Arkansas, Ohio, Tennessee, and Missouri Rivers all drain into the Mississippi. Its waters not only have some of the most traveled shipping channels in the United States, they're also home to odd creatures such as the paddlefish and the shovelnose sturgeon, remnants of a strange ancient lineage of fish. The Mississippi River is the biggest American flyway for ducks and geese, which travel and feed along its waters and wetlands on their migrations north and south.
- The Hudson River is a strange one: part river, part sea. Fresh water from the Adirondack Mountains flows down the river but, near the end, meets seawater pushing in

from the Atlantic Ocean. Incredibly productive, the river is home to millions of fish—marine and freshwater.

- You can sing "Way down upon the Suwannee River . . ." as you canoe on the Suwannee, a lazy, looping black water river that slowly moves to the Gulf of Mexico. The Suwannee begins in Georgia's Okefenokee Swamp, a wild place that is home to black bears, bobcats, and alligators. The river's black color comes from tree leaves that drop into its waters and release tannin—the same staining chemical that makes tea brown.

Water stained by tannin can be clearly seen in this photograph of Tahquamenon Falls, Michigan.

- The Sacramento and San Joaquin River systems provide more than half the water used in California. These rivers begin in the mountains, run through the Central Valley of California, merge in the delta region of San Francisco Bay, and flow into the Pacific Ocean.

As these facts illustrate, North America is rich in river resources. Whether you're drinking a glass of water in Atlanta, running a computer in Quebec, flushing a toilet in San Francisco, fishing in a river in Florida, bird-watching in Kansas, or washing clothes in Mexico City, you are relying on North America's rivers. These rivers shape the lives of plants, animals, and people all over the continent.

❧ 3 ❧
PHYSICAL FEATURES OF RIVERS AND STREAMS

"You cannot step twice in the same river," wrote the Greek philosopher Heraclitus 2,500 years ago. He was right. The river is a dynamic biome. Within seconds, water in which you wade flows past to some place beyond. A rainstorm can cause a desert river to swell from a tiny trickle to a dangerous wall of water—a flash flood—in minutes. In hours, floodwaters can cut through a muddy bank, causing a river to leap its banks and change course. And over hundreds and thousands of years, a river can wear down a mountain, carrying it grain by grain to the sea.

RIVER SOURCES

River water comes from a variety of sources. Snow and rain fall on rivers or fall onto the surrounding land and drain into rivers. Glaciers melt and pour into rivers. But the biggest water source for the world's rivers is out of sight—underground. This water is called groundwater. Groundwater comes from rain and melting snow that soak into the soil and move downward. Eventually, this water fills the spaces in gravel layers or porous sandstone and limestone. These water-holding rock layers are called aquifers. Underground, in aquifers, water can travel like a slow-moving river, at a rate of only inches a day.

Well: That's a Deep Subject Almost anywhere in the world, you can drill down and find water in an aquifer. But it's not always practical to do so. In deserts, an aquifer's top surface, called the water table, may be thousands of feet below ground. Water emerging from some aquifers feeds mountain springs. And where aquifers are tilted, groundwater flows downhill, building up so much pressure it squirts up and out of the ground. These formations, called artesian springs, can create Sahara Desert oases, where trees grow and camels drink.

Ancient Water The Ogallala Aquifer, which underlies the Great Plains, contains 1 quadrillion gallons (about 4 quadrillion liters) of water. It sounds like an almost endless supply, but it's not. People from South Dakota to Texas are using this water so quickly that scientists say 25 percent of it will be gone by the year 2020. Rainwater and melting snow percolate down through the soil and slowly refill the aquifer. But refilling it would take thousands of years: 6,000 years to fill the entire aquifer if it goes dry. Today, because the water level in the aquifer has dropped, Midwesterners have to drill their wells deeper to reach water.

From Groundwater to River Water Groundwater flowing out of springs often forms the start of a river: its headwaters. Groundwater can also flow into rivers farther along their course, where rivers cut deep into rock layers, exposing aquifers. An estimated one-half of the Mississippi River's volume comes from groundwater. River water can also flow *into* aquifers, replenishing them.

AGENTS OF CHANGE
Every day, all over the world, water wears down the land. This erosion helps create the strange Bad Lands of South

Dakota, the worn-down valleys of the Appalachians, and the splendid contours of the Grand Canyon.

The Big Three   Rivers sculpt the land through three main processes: erosion, transportation, and deposition. Once a river erodes—wears away—rock, soil, or other material, it transports it. A river carries this load of material, called silt or sediment, a distance ranging from a few inches to thousands of miles. The faster a river moves, the more sediment it can carry. Wherever the river slows down, especially at the river mouth, the river must drop, or deposit, its sediment load. In this way, the river can carry land, bit by bit, to the sea.

Wear and Tear   Rivers erode their banks through hydraulic action, abrasion, and corrosion. Hydraulic action—the force of the rushing water—sweeps away rock and soil, even boulders weighing 80 tons (72 metric tons)! Sediment-filled rivers work like sandpaper, abrading—scraping off—the rock over which they flow. (The same process smooths river pebbles as they tumble against one another.) Finally, water, because of its chemical properties, can corrode or dissolve rock such as sandstone. Every minute, 60 tons (54 metric tons) of dissolved matter pours over Niagara Falls. Both dissolved chemicals and sediment carried by river water can give it color, which may make rivers yellow, red, black, or white. As previously mentioned, the Suwannee River is black. China's Huang He River is yellow because of the fine, yellow soil it carries.

GOING WITH THE FLOW

The minute a raindrop lands on the earth, it tends to do one thing: go downhill. Gravity pulls the drop on this course. For most streams and rivers, downhill eventually leads to the ocean. But not all rivers make it there. Some dry up in the desert. Some feed into lakes. And others pour into underground caverns.

River Hide-and-Seek   Rivers are classified according to their flow. Permanent streams flow year-round. Intermittent streams flow only during certain seasons, after storms, or when snow melts in spring. Interrupted streams, such as the Santa Fe River in Florida, flow aboveground in places, then dip down and flow underground through coarse gravel or sand. These rivers may resurface elsewhere, flowing aboveground once again.

Straight, Curly, or Braided   As river water flows, it sculpts the channel in which it runs. This results in three main river shapes: straight stream, braided, and meandering. A straight stream river is just what you'd think: it runs in a fairly uncurved line. Braided streams, which look like braided strands of water, occur where there's plenty of soft, light sediment. These streams can't carry all the sediment they pick up, so they keep depositing it, forming gravel bars and sandbars. Strands of water weave among the bars. A third channel type, the meandering stream, loops and curves like a snake. This type is named for the Menderes River in Turkey, which flows in a looping path.

Why Rivers Loop and Curve   Water flowing downhill doesn't always flow in a straight line. It can develop a spiraling flow because of complicated physics that still has scientists somewhat baffled. This spiral action makes the river snake. Then, as water moves around a curve, the water on the outside of the curve goes faster than the water on the inside of the curve. This fast-flowing water picks up sediment, rounds the next curve, flows to the inside, slows

*A meandering stream snakes its way through
the Rocky Mountains of Colorado.*

down, and drops the sediment on the next bend. This process makes rivers curve more and more deeply over time.

RIVERINE LANDFORMS: DEEP, CURVY, AND WIDE
Rivers, as they flow, change the land—sometimes in dramatic ways.

Wonderful Waterfalls   Some of the greatest spectacles on earth are created by waterfalls, such as the longest waterfall on earth, Angel Falls, which cascades 3,213 feet (979 meters), and Niagara Falls, which has 670,000 gallons (2,500,000 liters) of water rushing over it every second. Waterfalls are created when water flowing over hard, resistant rock encounters softer rock. The soft rock is worn away, creating a drop: the falls. As water tumbles over a fall, it can curl underneath the fall's lip and cut away the supporting rock. This causes the lip of the waterfall to collapse. For this reason, waterfalls slowly move upstream over time. Ten thousand years ago, Niagara Falls was 6.8 miles (11 kilometers) farther downstream than it is today.

Oxbow Lakes A river that loops and curves across the land often has oxbow lakes scattered on either side of it. These form when the river is running high and fast. At

Niagara Falls is a popular attraction
for honeymooners and tourists alike!

those times, instead of quietly flowing around a curve, the river may take a shortcut, pushing straight ahead, forming a more direct route. This leaves a loop of the old channel abandoned. The abandoned loop, full of rainwater or leftover river water, becomes an oxbow lake, so named because of its bowlike shape.

Alluvial Fans   When a fast-moving stream, full of sediment, flows out onto a plain or into another river, it slows down. At slow speeds, the river can't carry as much sediment as it did when it was fast flowing. So the river drops its sediment load. This sediment forms an alluvial fan, a fan-shaped deposit that may be 10 or more miles (16 or more kilometers) wide.

Deltas   The word *delta* usually refers to an alluvial deposit that forms at a river's mouth where a river pours into the ocean. Deltas vary in shape, from the triangular delta of the Nile to the fan-shaped delta of the Niger to the bird's-foot-shaped delta of the Mississippi. But the landform got its name from the Nile's triangular delta, which is shaped like the Greek letter delta. By forming a delta, a river extends land out into the ocean. Over time, the river may change course near its mouth, creating several overlapping deltas, like layered fans. New Orleans sits on a delta built by the Mississippi River.

Down in the Valley   In dry regions, rivers cut deeply downward, forming steep-walled canyons and gorges. But in moist climates, rain and snow erode surrounding rock, too. This makes valleys change shape over millions of years. Young valleys are steep-sided, narrow, and V-shaped. Over time, rain and snow weaken the rock on each side of the river, so that it erodes and pieces slump, slide, and fall into

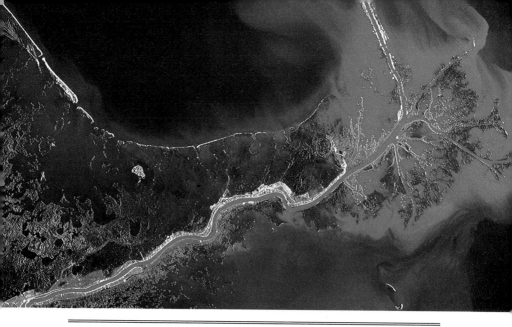

An infrared satellite photo shows silt (light blue)
deposited by the Mississippi River in its delta region.

the river and are carried away by the current. This widens
the valley into the characteristic mature valley, which has a
wide, level floor where the river can meander. Eventually,
when old, the valley's sides may be almost level, with a
broad plain where the river snakes along.

RIVERS, HEADWATER TO MOUTH

River characteristics change from their headwaters to their
mouths. While rivers may originate in lakes or where
springs feed into marshy wetlands, the "classic" stream
bubbles up in a mountain spring, creating a tumbling, clear,
rocky headwater stream. This stream's flow mixes with air,
resulting in a high oxygen content favorable for trout and
for insects, which hide in torrent moss or cling to stones.

Pickin' Up Speed   Downstream, as tributaries flow into it,
the stream grows in volume and width to create a midreach
stream. Here the streambed is less steep. The water appears

25

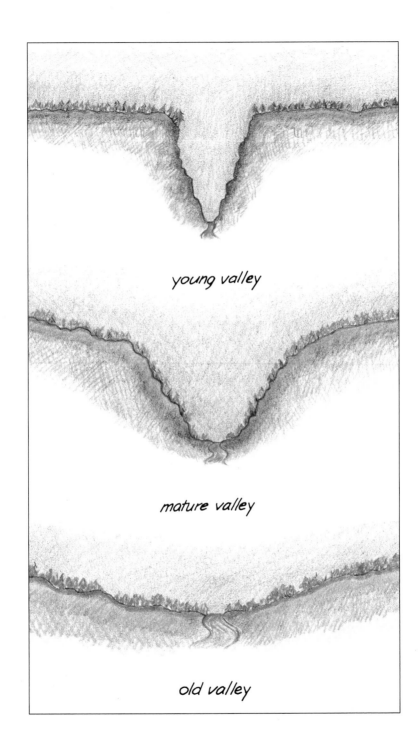

young valley

mature valley

old valley

calmer, although the current is swift and picks up additional sediment. Waterfalls, overhanging stream banks, sandbars, pools, and shallow, turbulent areas called riffles create a variety of aquatic habitats.

Slowing Down Sluggish, curvy, often muddy, base-level streams exist where the land has leveled off. These wandering streams, called bayous in Louisiana, seem to be in no hurry to get to the ocean. Their slow current allows plants to thickly colonize the riverbanks. During periodic flooding, stream water pours into surrounding meadows or forest, creating an area called a floodplain. Floodplains temporarily hold excess water and sometimes form wetlands. In these floodplains, streams deposit rich silt, which makes for good farmland, such as that which borders the Mississippi River and the Nile.

Rolling On Deep and usually muddy, large rivers don't loop across the land as base-level streams do. They have a more direct course yet still have a great habitat variety. Alligator gar, channel catfish, and paddlefish live here. These rivers often have dredged channels, dams, and locks, because they are used extensively for shipping.

End of the Road Near a river's mouth, where river water meets the ocean, is a place called the estuary. Here fresh water and salt water mix and freshwater and saltwater species mingle. Marshes often develop nearby.

Through the estuary, the river finally reaches its destination: the wide-open ocean. Along the way, the river has made its mark on the land over which it flows. You can see this even on the bottom of the ocean where, buried beneath the waves, lie the paths of ancient rivers that once ran over now sunken lands.

🐟 4 🐟
A WORLD OF
TINY CREATURES

Get close to a stream. Peer into its depths. Turn over a rock and stare at its sides. You'll find tiny creatures of many shapes and habits—some almost too strange to believe. Blackfly larvae, wormy and waving, catch food from the water's flow. Caddisfly larvae hide in hollow houses made of sticks and sand and stones. Water striders skate between water and air, sending messages with their feet. And beetles called water boatmen use their legs like oars to row and row and row.

VARIATIONS ON A STREAM THEME
For animals and plants, streams and rivers are places of variety. There are quiet backwaters with muddy bottoms, and rocky parts with a fast-moving flow. Trees and under-cut riverbanks create cool, shady spots, while exposed shallows are sunny and warm. Waterfalls mix water with air, creating oxygen-rich pools below. Stones provide crevices, shelter where tiny creatures can hide.

The Main Factors   Water quality is an important factor in aquatic creatures' lives. The water's temperature, volume, velocity, oxygen content, turbidity, and overall chemistry all affect their survival. For instance, turbidity—muddiness—can affect fish's gills or eyes. Africa's Zaire River is so

28

muddy that visibility is poor; some native fish send out electric currents to help them sense when an object is near. Temperature can be critical, too. Cutting trees that shade a river may warm the stream too much for cold-water trout to thrive. High water volume, such as occurs during flooding, may sweep fish eggs away, while a drop in water levels may expose fish eggs, which could dry and die in the sun. Water chemistry makes a difference as well. Snails, for instance, need calcium in the water so they can use it to build their spiral shells.

Velocity Even one factor, such as the water's velocity—its speed—can change greatly along the length of the stream. Stream waters may flow at a sedate 2 to 4 miles (3 to 6 kilometers) per hour but then speed up to 50 miles (81 kilometers) per hour over falls. And water speed is important. It determines how fast a fish must swim to stay in the same place and whether or not small organisms will be swept away.

Friction and the Invisible Layer Even in a small stretch of river, water moves at different speeds. Water in the middle of the river flows faster, while water on the bottom and sides flows more slowly. The reason for these different speeds is that friction with air, soil, or rock slows water down. Near the river bottom and around rocks, a thin layer of water slows almost to a stop. This invisible layer, only one-tenth inch (one-quarter centimeter) thick, is called the boundary layer. Here small, flattened creatures can thrive and not be swept away.

ADAPTATIONS OF RIVER DWELLERS
For most plants, surviving in a fast-flowing stream would be impossible. Flowing water easily breaks rigid stems and carries away leaves. But stream rocks are still slippery with

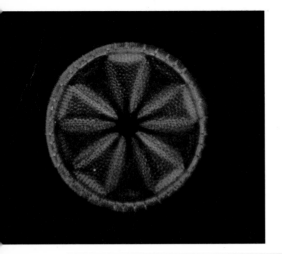
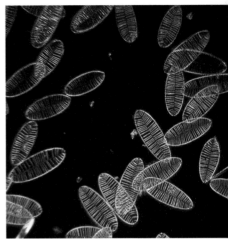

The silica shells of microscopic diatoms can be intricate.

plant life, which finds a place even here. Tiny, one-celled algae called diatoms encrust stones. Longer, stringy algae use holdfast cells to adhere to rocks. And clumps of liverworts and mosses cling to rocks, making miniature forests for tiny creatures such as mites, rotifers, protozoans, worms, and water bears. Like aquatic plants, river-dwelling animals have a variety of amazing adaptations.

Scrapers and Grazers   Algae may not be *your* idea of a good meal, but to a snail, they're a perfect food. Snails and freshwater limpets scrape algae off river rocks with rasping, tonguelike organs called radulae. Fish graze on algae, too. If there are enough algae-eaters, stream rocks may be almost bare!

Hook, Line, and Sucker   Those tiny blackflies that make life miserable for hikers from Minnesota to Montreal start out life as wriggling, wormlike larvae in streams. With the help of suction cups, blackfly larvae stick to rocks, using their head combs to catch tiny creatures from the current. Some blackfly species spin webs over stones in fast-flowing streams, then hang on, waiting for food to float by. Hooks on the legs of mayfly larvae help them hang on to algae-covered stones.

The Right Shape   Many stream creatures are streamlined. Smooth, torpedo-shaped trout, for instance, can swim upstream much more easily than a creature that is wide and catches the current's full force. Torrent beetles, which stick close to rocks, have low-profile shells, like tiny sports cars. Stonefly larvae, with their flattened bodies, can stick close to rocks, feeding on algae. Water pennies are flat, with tiny spines that help their body hug rocks.

Filter Feeders and Detritus Delight   Animals such as mayfly larvae, stonefly larvae, and freshwater clams drink in water and filter out edible tidbits. What they're eating is detritus. Detritus is part dead—plant parts, leaves, dead animals, droppings, and so on. And it's part alive, with microorganisms such as bacteria, diatoms, photosynthetic flagellates, ciliates, nematodes, and others. Some of these microorganisms make their own food, some feed on the decaying material, and others are tiny predators, which feed on tiny prey.

Blood Drinkers and Diving Spiders   In streams, as every-where else, certain creatures feed on other animals. Leeches and flatworms feed on snails, worms, and occasionally mammals such as humans, too. Stonefly larvae and dobson-fly larvae capture small insects and sometimes tiny fish. Fishing spiders have a hairy coat that traps air, keeping them dry as they dive. Remaining underwater for as long as forty-five minutes, these spiders catch and eat insect larvae.

Catch My Drift? At night, aquatic insects rise from the stream bottom and float up to several yards downstream. Scientists call this drift. The exact reason for drift is unknown. But fish wait for drifting insects and gulp them down. With all these creatures drifting downstream each night, it's a wonder there are still any insects left upstream. Some creatures can actually swim back upstream, while others, such as insect nymphs, turn into adult insects that can fly upstream and lay eggs, renewing their population.

Life Is Short As stream-dwelling larvae, mayflies live an entire year underwater. But once they molt and emerge as adult winged mayflies, they only live one day. During that day, their only "job" is to breed and lay eggs. After that task, they die. Flying swarms emerge and die in staggering numbers. One summer, a snowplow had to be used to clear a several-foot-thick layer of dead mayflies off a bridge near the Mississippi River!

The Amazing Caddisfly Wrapped in a sticky web decorated by sand, sticks, and leaves, caddisfly larvae hide from predators. (They're named for caddis-men: old-time traveling salesmen who pinned ribbons, cloth, and braids on their coats to show for sale.) In fast-moving water, some caddisflies create heavy cases covered with tiny stones, which weigh them down. In calmer waters, other caddisflies build diamond-shaped sand cases or live in squared-off plant stems. Most caddisflies graze on algae. But a few build funnel-shaped nets for catching food. And others swing on anchor lines into the current, using their hairy legs to catch food from the passing flow.

"Sneaky" Clams Freshwater clams have a strange habit. They disperse the population by sending their offspring hitchhiking! The adult clam may wait until a fish swims by. Or it may lure one with flesh that looks like a delicious little fish, complete with an eyespot and tail. Either way, when the real fish swim close, the adult clam squirts out lots of tiny baby clams. The baby clams clamp onto the fish's gills and fins. They ride along, then drop off in a new area.

Surface Skaters   Aquatic insects have evolved some fantastic ways of moving. Water striders skate along the stream's surface. And when they want to send a message to other water striders, they tap their feet on the water, sending out ripples in the stream. Water boatmen use their thickened, oarlike legs to row. Whirligig beetles whirl in circles near the surface; no one can say exactly why. And diving beetles dive. These beetles breathe from bubbles tucked underneath their wing covers. Tiny beetles may need only one bubble to last a lifetime!

Water's surface tension allows a water strider to skate atop a stream.

FROM TREE LEAVES TO TROUT

Next time you dine on a delicious trout, remember to thank a tree. And a fungus. And a bacterium. And some insects, too. Because food for wild fish doesn't come in flakes from a fish food can. Instead, many tiny, unglamorous creatures play a role in the development of fish.

Leaves and Shredders   In many streams, leaves and other plant pieces that fall into the water are an important source of food. In shaded mountain streams, they may provide up to 99 percent of the basic plant material in the stream. When a leaf falls into the water, bacteria and fungi begin breaking it down, causing it to decay. At the same time, creatures nicknamed "shredders"—crane-fly larvae, stone-fly nymphs, crayfish, and some caddisfly larvae—tear apart, or shred, the leaves and eat them, fungi, bacteria, and all. Shredders' droppings and uneaten food particles become food for other creatures, such as snails and worms. And the shredders themselves become meals for other insects and for trout.

Strands in the Aquatic Web   As you can tell from the process described above, each insect, snail, leaf, fungus, and alga plays an important role in the stream's ecology. The life of each organism in the stream is connected to the lives of the others. And they are connected to the surrounding land-scape as well. If streamside trees are removed, there will be no leaves to feed the algae and fungi and the shredders, and without shredders, there's no food for fish. Like the tale of the battle that was lost all for the want of a horseshoe nail, the stream needs each and every one of its living and non-living components.

🐟 5 🐟
FISH AND THE
RIVER COMMUNITY

Lurking in the waters of the mighty Mississippi is a fish so big it's been known to take on an alligator and win. Alligator gars reach almost 10 feet (3 meters) in length and usually dine on fish, not gators. But this Mississippi giant is just one of the sizable creatures that live in and around rivers and streams. From leaping fish and diving birds to basking turtles and slithering snakes, rivers and riverbanks are packed with wildlife.

RIVERINE FISH

You can tell a lot about a fish by its "smile." Fish whose mouths are turned upward are generally surface feeders. They feed on things that fall into the water or live near the water's surface. A fish whose mouth has a downward curve is likely to be a bottom feeder. It slurps up food that drops on the river bottom. A fish with a mouth pointing forward may eat fish or other food items found neither at the top nor the bottom but in the middle layer of the river.

Fish Self-Defense   If you're a fish, it's wise to keep an eye out for bigger fish and for fish-eating birds such as herons and kingfishers. But beware of smaller creatures, too! Tiny, newly hatched fish become the prey of insect larvae, fishing spiders, and even crayfish. If predators

35

draw near, fish stay still to avoid being seen or dart to safer waters. Some fish avoid predators by appearing difficult to eat. Sticklebacks and sunfish have spines that can be a real mouthful. Speckled madtoms, a type of catfish found in America's Midwest, have spines that are not only prickly but poisonous!

Gills, Swim Bladders, and Lines   Fish have a wide variety of adaptations for aquatic life. Instead of lungs, they have gills, which extract oxygen from water. And they adjust the air in their balloonlike swim bladders to keep them buoyant instead of sinking down. Running along each side of a fish is an organ called the lateral line, which is basically a long tube with holes in it. Fluid flowing in and out of the tube triggers hairs. These hairs indicate the pressure and turbulence of the surrounding water. This helps fish avoid running into nearby objects or other fish. In addition, catfish sport whiskerlike barbels that help them detect prey.

Fish and More Fish   The period when fish lay eggs and fertilize them is called spawning season. This period lasts from a few days to a few weeks. During this time, some male fish turn bright colors to attract females. The jaw of the sockeye salmon becomes long and distinct, making it look rather fearsome to humans but perhaps attractive to female salmon. Some female fish give birth to live young, but most lay eggs. Once eggs are laid, egg-eating predators move in quickly. Fortunately, fish usually lay large numbers of eggs, so some do survive to be fertilized and to hatch. Male sculpins, bluntnose minnows, and sunfish stay around and chase off predators until their fertilized eggs hatch.

Nest Builders   Like birds, many fish build nests—not in trees, of course, but on the bottom of a river or stream. River chubs and cutlip minnows build nests by carrying small

GO FISH-WATCHING!

Although not as popular as bird-watching, fish-watching is fun, too. Bring a notebook, a pencil, and binoculars if you have them. Walk along the bank of a stream or river. Find a place where you can see into the water. Look for the following sights:

- Shadows on the bottom—you may see a fish's shadow before you can see its body, which blends in with the background.
- Rings and bubbles on the water's surface. This may indicate small fish are feeding below.
- Fish eggs, which can be in pancake-shaped masses, floating free in the water, scattered on pebbly stream bottoms, or assembled in long jellylike ribbons.
- Fish resting under aquatic plants, stream banks, or in deep pools.

Watch each fish's behavior. Is it resting? Hiding? Building a nest? Take notes on your observations. For more information on fish-watching, read *Fish Watching* by C. Lavett Smith (Comstock, 1994).

pebbles in their mouths to the nest site. There they pile them up into a mound. In Michigan, a scientist watched a chub pile up 7,050 pebbles to make its 3-foot- (almost 1-meter-) wide nest! Fish called sticklebacks build nests out of plants glued together with sticky fluids made by their kidneys. Other fish choose an easier method, simply using their tails to dig nesting pits out of gravel or sand.

Baby Doesn't Look Like Dad   As they grow older, some fish change not just in size but in overall appearance, too. They may change their feeding habits as well. When they are young, suckers—a kind of fish—have upturned mouths to feed near the water's surface. Yet older suckers have downward-pointing mouths and swim closer to the river bottom. By having different lifestyles, the adult fish and the young fish do not compete with each other for food.

Pool Dwellers and Riffle Riders   Look along a stream's surface and you'll find the water is calm in some areas and turbulent in others. The shallow, rocky, turbulent areas are called riffles. Calmer, deeper areas are called pools. Some fish, such as perch, smallmouth bass, sunfish, and a variety of minnows, prefer pools. Riffles are the domain of sculpins, darters, longnose dace, and madtom catfish. Oddly enough, although pebbles and sediment constantly move along the stream, the riffles and pools stay in place. Pebbles simply migrate from one riffle to the next. So these species of fish can be found in the same place on the river, year after year.

Creatures of Two Worlds   Some fish and other fishlike species spend part of their lives in rivers and part in oceans as well. Catadromous species, such as American eels, migrate from rivers to the ocean to spawn. Salmon, shad, and lampreys are anadromous species, meaning they do the reverse, migrating from the ocean to rivers to spawn. Salmon hatch in streams, then travel downstream to the ocean, where they spend several years growing large and fat. That fat helps them on their long journey, as much as 2,000 or more miles (3,200 or more kilometers), back to their home stream, where they lay eggs, then die. During the whole journey, fighting their way upstream, salmon navigate by smell and do not eat.

OTHER RESIDENTS, PLUS VISITORS

Fish aren't the only creatures that live in streams and rivers. Bald eagles, otters, turtles, salamanders, kingfishers, and other creatures can be found in and along streams and rivers, too. These animals may depend on streams and rivers for food, water, shelter, and a place to raise their young.

Watch Those Pincers!   If you're wading in a stream or turning over stream rocks, keep your eyes peeled. You might encounter the strong pinching claws of a crayfish. Crayfish scuttle out from behind or under rocks and grab food. Collecting crayfish, or crawdads, used to be a favorite pastime for kids. A basket of these tiny relatives of the lobster and shrimp makes a good meal.

Tricky Tongue and Others   Human fishermen aren't the only ones who attract fish with bait. Alligator snapping turtles sit still on the river bottom, unobtrusive in their dull-colored shells. They wave a red, wormlike part of their tongues to attract fish. Once a fish swims near, *crunch!* The turtle's jaws snap tight on its fish dinner. Other reptiles, such as snakes, may live almost their entire lives in streams and rivers. And rivers are home to amphibians, including newts, frogs, and the gigantic hellbender salamander, which can be over 2 feet (61 centimeters) long.

A small fish is about to become a meal for this crayfish.

HOW OLD IS THAT FISH?

In this activity, you can determine the age of a fish, the same way scientists do.

Here are the materials you will need:

• fish scales

• magnifying glass or microscope

Obtain several scales from one or more dead fish. (You might ask at a fish market or grocery store for these.)

Use a magnifying glass or microscope to look closely at the fish's scales. Can you see the rings, called circuli? Unlike humans, fish continue growing

This close-up of fish scales shows rings, or circuli.

their entire lives. As they grow, fish add rings to their scales, as a tree does to its trunk. In early spring, when food is abundant, fish grow rapidly. Their scale rings grow wide apart. By fall, the food supply tapers off, and the last rings are small, close together, and sometimes incomplete. The end of the close circuli marks a year, or annulus. The next spring, the wide rings formed may cut across the ones from the previous year.

Scientists study these rings to gauge a fish's age. But irregular patterns in circuli can also mark other events. Floods, unusual weather, spawning, competition with other fish—any activity that might affect growth—also change the ring pattern. So by studying fish, scientists can find out about living conditions in the stream where the fish live.

Can you guess how old the fish is by the scales you examine? Do the circuli vary much in size? If not, the fish may have been raised in captivity and have had a constant food supply.

The Daffy Dipper and Other Birds One of the most famous stream dwellers is the dipper, a little brown bird that nips in and out of the current. Dippers use their wings as flippers. At times, the dipper is completely submerged, foraging for aquatic insects. Another common bird of streams and rivers is the kingfisher. You might hear one's rattling cry as it flies along the river's length, at times skimming close to the water. In flight or from a tree limb lookout, a kingfisher scans the water for fish, then dives in to grasp one in its beak. Other common birds found along rivers and streams include green herons, blue herons, mergansers, and wood ducks. Seasonally, streams also attract small birds that dine on flying insects that have just emerged from their aquatic, larval stage.

Otters and Others Romping on a riverbank or sliding down snow into a stream, river otters are playful, sleek, sociable animals. Their webbed feet, strong tails, and flexible bodies make them good swimmers. Otters feed on frogs, crayfish, small birds, mice, and fish, and dig their dens into riverbanks. Other mammals frequent streams as well. Beavers dam streams to make the deepwater pools they prefer. During salmon runs, brown bears may spend almost all day standing in streams, eating salmon that are trying to swim upstream.

THE STREAM COMMUNITY

Living together, the animals and plants of a stream or river form a community. Ecologists—scientists who study natural communities—diagram these kinds of relationships in a food web. A food web shows which species eat which species within a community. It also shows how energy flows through the community. Energy from the sun is used by a plant to make leaves. A leaf is eaten by an insect, and

*River otters are playful acrobats, continually
sliding and tumbling into the water.*

part of the leaf's energy is stored in the insect's body. A
trout eats the insect, and part of the insect's energy becomes
part of the trout. And so energy travels through the community, although much is lost as heat in each step of the
process. A food web demonstrates the interconnectedness
of riverine plants and animals.

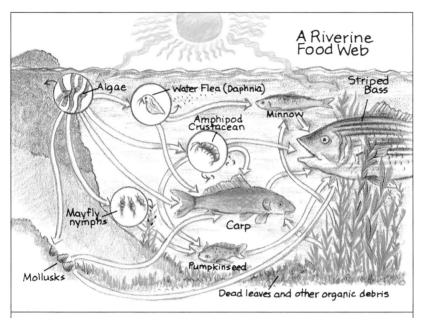

A Riverine Food Web

Algae
Water Flea (Daphnia)
Striped Bass
Amphipod Crustacean
Minnow
Mayfly nymphs
Carp
Mollusks
Pumpkinseed
Dead leaves and other organic debris

This food web shows how energy flows through a river community. For example, energy from the sun is used by plants. Energy from the plants flows to the minnow that eats them. Some of the minnow's energy then passes to the bass that eats it.

Dazzling Diversity   Compared to lakes, streams have high animal diversity—a large number of different kinds of animals. Scientists believe this is because streams and rivers offer such a variety of conditions, including riffles, pools, waterfalls, meanders, and backwaters. A different type of animal may adapt to live under each different set of conditions. Generally, the larger the river, the more habitat variations it offers and the more species it can contain.

Streamside Worlds   Riparian habitat is very important to wildlife inside and outside the stream. Tree leaves falling in the water provide an important food source in the aquatic food web. Trees, tree roots, and plants on riverbanks help catch soil carried by rain running off the land. Without

· THE STRANGE CASE OF THE HATCHERY FISH ·

In North America, so many people love fishing that there aren't enough wild fish to satisfy them. So fishery biologists raise fish in captivity and release them into the wild. You'd think that releasing hatchery-raised fish into a stream would make fishing better. But sometimes that's not the case.

When hatchery fish and wild fish meet, it's like they don't speak the same language. One biologist described it this way: "It's like watching a motorcycle gang invade a quiet rural town." The hatchery fish don't know the wild fish's rules and social signals. As a result, the hatchery fish blunder in and push the wild fish out of their territories into places with poorer food sources. Hatchery-raised fish take the good spots but aren't very good at foraging. The result is that neither the hatchery fish nor the wild fish do well.

Scientists are now beginning to recognize that populations of fish, even of the same species, are not all the same. A population of wild fish living in a stream or lake adapts to the conditions of that particular habitat. When these fish are mixed with and interbred with wild fish from another river, they may result in fish less able to survive conditions in a particular wild river. Today, fishery managers are working to breed hatchery fish that are more like wild fish in behavior. They are also being more cautious about introducing fish populations to the wild.

these plants to slow runoff, rain erodes banks and muddy water can pour into rivers, drastically affecting aquatic life. As you can see, all the components of the river community, from the insects to the fish to the turtles, otters, and trees, are important to the health of a stream.

❧ 6 ❧
ESTUARY: WHERE RIVER MEETS THE SEA

Underwater, in an estuary, where river meets the sea, there's a strange concert going on. Oyster toadfish, lumpy, with bulging eyes, sit on the mud and grunt. Shrimp snap their pincers. Crabs rasp their claws. Croakers squeeze their swim bladders: "*Croak!*" Black drums crunch on oyster shells. Sea robins chirp like birds instead of fish. And at night, a light show starts, with the blue flashing of comb jellies and the green sparkling of plankton afloat. The entire concert may be witnessed only by a scallop, with its forty blue eyes on stalks. But if you're quiet, you may see and hear it all, even above water, from shore or from a boat.

A RICH BUT HARSH ENVIRONMENT

An estuary is an ecotone—a place where two biomes, in this case river and ocean, mix. As such, it shares some of the physical features and organisms of both biomes. But it also has some interesting characteristics of its own.

Marshes, Mudflats, and More Estuaries form where rivers meet the ocean, usually but not always in a bay, a body of water that is set off from the ocean. Around an estuary or scattered within it may be salt marshes, mudflats, sandbars, and spits of land. In tropical areas, mangrove

Much of the southwestern tip of Florida is covered with mangrove swamps that contain red mangrove trees like these.

swamps may grow nearby. All these habitats influence the lives of estuarine animals and plants. Birds, crabs, fish, and other species move back and forth between these habitats during their daily activities.

The Mixing Bowl   An estuary is something of a mixing bowl. The river's flow pushes fresh water out the river mouth. Ocean tides push salt water inland. Together these forces mix the fresh water and salt water, creating brackish water, which has a medium salinity, or saltiness. But the mixing job is by no means complete. Much of the fresh water simply floats on top of the denser, salty ocean water. How well the salt water and fresh water mix depends on the shape of the estuary and its currents. The estuary's salinity can vary hour to hour, day to day, season to season, and even location to location. These variations are caused by seasonal floods, daily tides, and the rotation of the earth.

The fluctuating salinities are difficult for most animals to withstand, but those that are adapted to them flourish.

Why Salt Matters   Most saltwater creatures would die in fresh water. Most freshwater creatures would die if put in salt water. Why? Because animals and plants are made mostly of water. Their cells' activities are regulated by water and salts made of chloride, magnesium, potassium, and other elements. To maintain an equilibrium—the same salt concentration inside and outside the cell—water tends to move in or out of a cell. But so much water may flow in that the cell bursts, or so much water may flow out that the cell collapses. If this happens in an animal's body, it dies. Aquatic animals are adapted to balance the salts and water in their cells, for their particular environment—salt water or fresh water. Only a few species can survive a shift in the salinity of their environment.

Nutrient Soup   By the time a river reaches the sea, it has slowed down and already dropped most of its bigger particles upstream. What it deposits in estuaries is fine silt and detritus. Detritus becomes a part of an estuary's rich "nutrient soup." Decaying, algae-covered marsh grasses also wash off salt marshes and into the estuary, adding to the estuary's nutrient richness. In some estuaries, tides may bring in ocean sediments, too. In the constantly mixing environment of an estuary, these nutrients stay suspended in the water, available to animals. This mixing also keeps oxygen levels high, which helps animals use the available nutrients.

ESTUARINE PLANTS AND ANIMALS
From worms that wiggle in the mud and sand, to fish that cruise the muddy waters, to birds that wade along their shallows, estuaries are filled with wildlife. Pipefish, with

bodies as skinny as their name suggests, feed along eelgrass beds. Amphipods, shrimp, and sea spiders clamber among oysters and clams. Anemones' waving tentacles and worms' feather duster plumes gather tidbits from the passing flow.

Salt Strategies   Most estuaries are quiet places, protected from the strongest ocean waves. But for animals, they can be a challenging environment, mostly because of the fluctuating salinity. Mussels close their shells when the water is too salty or too dilute. Worms and amphipods dig deeper in the mud and wait until unfavorable conditions change. Microscopic plankton, which are adapted to specific salinity ranges, flow with the water as it moves. Blue crabs don't shift with the tides, because their bodies change chemically to cope.

Plants and Plant-Eaters   Estuaries have their own plant life, but none of it is showy or large. Microscopic plants called phytoplankton drift in with ocean waters. Algae thrive as a living green frosting on mud, eelgrass, or even sunken trash. Eelgrasses, which aren't grasses at all but a type of herb, grow in beds of waving blades where fish hide. Worms, clams, and scallops drink in a soup of nutritious phytoplankton and detritus. Other larger plants grow in salt marshes, where aquatic animals can eat them at high tide.

Gobies and Other Gobblers   In estuaries, many fish and other animals are predators. Tiny fish called gobies eat mites, shrimp, and even barnacles. Flatfish such as flounder feed on worms, shrimp, and small fish. Comb jellies, transparent creatures similar to jellyfish, sweep up oyster larvae and other tiny prey. Herons and other birds eat snails, fish,

48

and shrimp. And during low tides, shorebirds wander mudflats, feeding on worms and other burrowers.

The Burrowers Burrowing is a popular habit among estuarine animals. Hairy sea cucumbers remain buried, with only their tentacles aboveground, catching food tidbits. Mantis prawns, also known as "shrimp snappers," lie mud-covered, with only their eyes exposed. When a small

A mantis prawn (top) lurks in its burrow, waiting for prey to pass by. When a sea cucumber (bottom) hides in the sand, only its tentacles will show.

shrimp or fish happens by, the mantis prawn's large, spiny claws reach up from the mud to snatch it.

Wonderful Worms If you're a fan of squirmy, wormy creatures with strange habits, you'll like estuaries. Estuaries and the bays that surround them are home to leafy paddle worms, clam worms, twelve-scaled worms, two-gilled blood worms, polydora mud worms, Gould's peanut worms, lug worms, bamboo worms, and even ice cream cone worms! (Although these creatures have worm names and wormy looks, not all are closely related to earthworms.) The ice cream cone worm makes its almost 2-inch- (5-centimeter-) long tube out of a single layer of sand grains cemented by mucus. Out of this cone, it extends its feeding tentacles to sweep up food. Down in their burrows, lug worms eat sand, digesting any edible tidbits between the grains, then scoot back up to the sand surface to squirt out the leftover sand.

THE ESTUARY IS THEIR OYSTER

Estuaries are a haven for oysters, which feed by filtering out detritus from water. Many oysters grow together, forming oyster beds. All along the eastern coast of the United States, people harvest oysters for food. In Japan, people harvest them for pearls, which are made by an oyster to wall off material that irritates its soft, sensitive flesh.

Oyster Enemies Even with their hard shells, oysters are a sought-after food. Sea stars use their strong, sucker-equipped arms to force open oyster shells. Fish called black drums feed on oysters by crushing their shells with teeth deep in their throats. Oystercatchers, which are birds with long, strong, red beaks, force their beaks between an oyster's two shells and cut the muscles that hold the shells closed. Then they can lay the oyster open and dine. Oyster drills—which look like tiny whelks or conchs—try another approach. They use chemicals to soften the oyster's shell and a toothed organ called a radula to drill into the soft spot. Alternately drilling and softening, eventually they make a hole through which they then can insert their tonguelike proboscises and feed.

Oyster Neighbors   Like coral reefs, oyster beds have a variety of inhabitants. Anemones and barnacles attach to oyster shells. Atlantic slipper limpets, a type of snail, grow among the oysters, too. Shrimp and small fish dart between them. Some neighbors can be a nuisance: tiny crab larvae enter oyster shells and grow up inside, which doesn't leave much room for the oyster. The crab emerges as an adult. Minuscule boring sponges settle onto living or dead oyster shells and use sulfuric acid to bore in. They make tiny passageways that can lead to the disintegration of the oyster's entire shell.

Competing Communities   The survival of an oyster community can be threatened by many factors in addition to predators and parasites. Oysters are susceptible to fungal and bacterial diseases. Polydora mud worms, if they become too numerous, may smother the reef with their tubes and discarded mud. River floodwaters or strong waves from hurricanes can wash suffocating sediment over the bed. And pollution from factories and other human developments can kill oysters, too.

THE BIG PICTURE
Three-quarters of the shellfish and seafood we eat depend on estuaries and salt marshes during early stages in their lives because their eggs are laid there or their young grow

up there. Fish such as salmon migrate through estuaries on their way to and from rivers. And striped bass, flounder, clams, oysters, and other food species can spend their entire lives within estuarine waters.

But estuaries are home to people, too. Major cities border on estuaries in North America's Chesapeake Bay, Delaware Bay, San Francisco Bay, Apalachicola Bay, Galveston Bay, and Upper New York Bay. One reason cities exist so close to estuaries is that estuaries and bays are centers for shipping between inland rivers and the sea. Oil refineries, nuclear power stations, and heavy industries also are often sited in estuaries to be close to ships that can bring supplies and take away products. Many industries also need large supplies of water for cooling and a place to discharge wastewater when their production processes are finished.

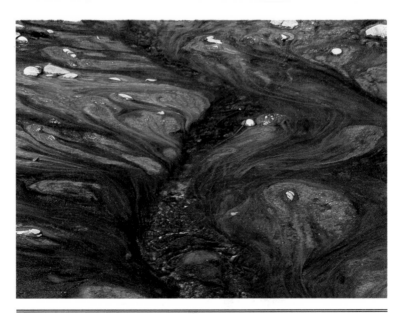

Algae on the water's surface can block the sunlight aquatic plants need to live.

Blooming Problems   One of the most common pollutants entering estuaries is human sewage. After all, estuaries are a common site for cities. When sewage enters the water, planktonic algae feed on the nitrogen-rich broth. They quickly increase in numbers, "blooming" on the surface of the water and blocking light needed by other plants. Aquatic plants in shallow waters die out, and with them go creatures that live in these waters, such as pipefish and croakers. The fish eating those fish decline, and the overall health of the estuary may be threatened.

Estuarine Pollution   Rivers themselves may bring in pollution, too. And locally, pollution from industry and runoff of fertilizers, oil, gasoline, pesticides, and other products from developed areas can harm estuarine animals and plants. Once it was believed that toxic wastewater dumped into estuaries would quickly be flushed out to sea. But now it is known that this kind of pollution may circulate in an estuary for a much longer time and accumulate in its sediments. Even dilute pollutants can build up to toxic levels. Another threat to estuarine health is the dredging, paving, draining, filling, or other alteration of mudflats and salt marshes. Damaging these habitats can deprive an estuary of important nutrients.

Helping Hands   Today, however, many people are working to ensure that estuaries are clean and healthy. In Delaware, for instance, government officials and citizen volunteers have banded together to battle the Delaware estuary's pollution troubles. Volunteers are mapping creeks that pour into the estuary and testing their water quality. County soil conservation officials are planting plants to stabilize riverbanks and prevent erosion. Citizen groups are stenciling storm drains with messages informing people that these drains lead straight into the estuary and asking them not to dump pollutants in the drains. Environmental groups are producing films, displays, and other media to educate the public about the estuary's troubles and possible solutions to those problems. And volunteers are even learning how to take care of injured wildlife in the event of an oil spill. With all these people at work, the future of the Delaware estuary is in good hands.

ᔫ 7 ᔭ
PEOPLE AND
RIVERS AND STREAMS

One of America's most famous writers, Samuel Clemens, took his pen name from a river term. "Mark Twain!" a lookout would yell to a Mississippi River boat captain if the water was almost too shallow to pass. Mark Twain's writings, including *The Adventures of Huckleberry Finn*, chronicle the mixed emotions people have toward rivers. They love them, fear them, and depend on them in a host of different ways.

RIVERS: TOO CLOSE FOR COMFORT?

People crowd close to river edges. They want access to river fishing, river shipping, river recreation, and water for drinking, washing, farming, and industry. But by developing land near rivers, people leave themselves vulnerable to natural floods. And unwise development can make natural flooding worse.

Faster Flows When land is paved for shopping malls, houses, or other development, rain can no longer soak into the soil. Instead, it flows quickly over the pavement and pours into streams, which then swell rapidly in size. This aggravates flooding. But what can make the problem even worse is what people then do to protect their riverside development and farms. They build levees and concrete

• FLOODS: THE GOOD AND BAD •

In 1993, the Mississippi River swelled with rain and jumped its banks. It flooded fifty-five towns, swept away houses, displaced 62,000 families, and smothered farm fields with sand. Unusually heavy rains caused the flooding, which occurred on the upper portions of the Mississippi, from Minnesota south to Illinois and west to Nebraska. Farther downstream, where the river channel is wider, flooding was less of a problem.

Boats replaced cars on flooded streets.

But upstream, it was the worst flooding in a century or more. Fifty people died and $12 billion of property was destroyed. Levees broke under the force of the rushing water. For weeks, the Red Cross, the Salvation Army, federal agencies, neighbors, strangers, and even volunteers from other parts of the country banded together, pumping water out of buildings, filling and stacking sandbags to try to keep back the floods, and sheltering and feeding people displaced by the floods. Floodwaters wiped out drinking water supplies and sewage backed up into the streets. When the waters receded, what hadn't been washed away by the floods was covered with mud and slime. A woman pulled back the covers of her bed only to find it filled with mud and earthworms.

At times like those, it's hard to remember that floods have their advantages. Flooding rivers deposit sediment, creating rich soil. That's one reason productive farms hug the Mississippi's edges in the first place. Flood-carried sediment builds deltas outward, creating new and valuable land. And floodwaters create and maintain wetlands and mudflats, where many species of wildlife thrive. Overall, the Mississippi flood of 1993 was a boon for many wildlife species, particularly fish, which spawned in the newly flooded areas.

But the fact remains that people suffered greatly. Nevertheless, many resolved to rebuild after the flood. Meanwhile, engineers, conservationists, and flood experts nationwide called for the government to give people incentives to move out of the flood danger areas, instead of just giving them money to rebuild in the floodplain. Some towns and some individuals did make the decision to move to higher ground. But most of the government disaster aid went to rebuild levees and help people rebuild in the floodplain.

Some government money also went to new, creative programs to help solve the flood problems. The government paid farmers $100 million *not* to farm 110,000 acres of farmland vulnerable to flooding. For the farmers, it was a good deal, because they got paid to abandon their flooded farms, many of which were buried in sand. For the government, it was a good deal, too. These abandoned farms will become wetlands where the river can spread out during floods and some of the floodwater can be absorbed. This will help prevent flooding in other, more populated areas and eliminate the need for some levees. And for fish, ducks, and other wildlife, these wetlands will serve as much-needed habitat.

channels to control the river's flow, to prevent flooding, and to stabilize the banks. This may work for small floods in their area. But stream water running through narrow, smooth channels gains speed and force, making downstream flooding worse.

Floodplains in the Future   Today, many people are recognizing the wisdom of letting rivers "do their thing"—roam in natural riverbeds and spread out over natural floodplains. Unlike concrete channels, natural riverbeds provide nutrients, variety, and shelter—rocks, overhangs, and plants where aquatic creatures hide. Protecting and restoring riparian habitat, including wetlands, furnishes a home for wildlife. It also provides a place where floodwater can spread out and soak in. New laws recognize that in some places, it may not make sense to build and rebuild near rivers where flooding danger is high. But the economic and personal investments people have made in riverside developments often make it difficult to abandon them now.

THE QUESTION OF DAMS

For thousands of years, people have harnessed the energy of flowing water. By using waterwheels, people made water do the work of grinding grain and irrigating fields. Today, river water turns turbines that generate electricity. This form of energy is called hydroelectric power.

Pros and Cons   Unlike power plants that burn coal, oil, or peat, hydroelectric generators do not create air pollution. They don't produce dangerous, radioactive by-products as do nuclear power plants. But hydroelectric power does have major disadvantages. When a dam is built, a huge lake backs up behind the dam. The lake floods large areas, which may include towns, villages, farmland, sacred tribal sites, and wilderness. Dam building and associated development also change a river's character. The speed, temperature, and oxygen level of the water are altered, killing off many aquatic species. Dams also affect rafting, fishing, and farming downstream. It's no wonder these massive engineering projects, with their multibillion-dollar price tags, have become so controversial. In North America, most major dammable rivers have already been dammed. So the political and legal battles over damming the remaining free-running rivers have grown particularly fierce. In Quebec, Canada, the native Cree people and environmentalists are battling to oppose the James Bay Project, the largest hydroelectric project in the world.

Brown bears are one of many species that depend on salmon.
Bears fatten up for winter by eating rich salmon meat.

Up a Stream Without a Ladder Salmon, which migrate up rivers and streams in order to spawn, are endangered by the building of dams. Once plentiful, salmon are now comparatively rare in the dammed rivers of the Pacific Northwest and Atlantic coast. Their decline has impacted eagles, bears, and sport and commercial fishermen, who catch the salmon as they race to spawn. And for some Native American tribes whose economy and culture center around salmon, the loss of fish has been particularly damaging. Over the last few decades, millions of dollars have been spent creating fish ladders that help salmon get upstream, past dams. These ladders, which run along the sides of dams, allow fish to slowly spiral upward, jumping up small, water-covered "steps" as they would up natural waterfalls, in order to get beyond the dam. But overall, despite high-tech efforts to save them, the salmon have drastically declined.

POLLUTION

Rivers aboveground and below ground are threatened by pollution of many sorts. In the Ozarks, toxic lead and other pollutants from mining leach into streams. On Cape Cod, millions of gallons of toxins—poisonous substances—dumped on a military base have percolated down into the soil and are seeping into water supplies. Five main types of pollution endanger rivers and streams: sewage, industrial toxins, thermal pollution, polluted runoff, and excess sediment from erosion.

Slimy Sewage When lots of animals get together—cows in feedlots or people in cities and towns—the poop can really pile up. It's a smelly problem as old as civilization. (Even in the ancient city of Pompeii, there were indoor toilets—some were seven-seaters!) Throughout history, many people have "solved" the sewage problem by dumping it into streams and rivers, which carry it away. People down-stream, however, have never been particularly thrilled with that solution—especially because human sewage often contains disease-causing microbes.

A Bacterial Feast   Although streams can handle small amounts of sewage, large amounts cause bacteria to multiply rapidly, using up the stream's oxygen and suffocating other aquatic creatures. Algae also grow thickly, blocking light from other aquatic plants, causing them to die.

Better, But Not Perfect   Today, most people in the United States have access to a system to handle sewage. Water treatment plants clean water before it's released into streams. Septic tanks allow sewage to decompose before it's released into the soil. But many places in the world are not so fortunate. In some cities and towns, open ditches of sewage run along streets and pour directly into rivers. Even in the United States and Canada, some treatment plants are overloaded. After rainstorms, when water volume is high, the plant may not be able to handle the load. It may dump untreated sewage directly into rivers. And septic systems, if not properly maintained, may leak sewage into soils and streams.

Toxins and Temperatures   More than 500 million pounds (225 million kilograms) of toxins are dumped by industry into lakes, streams, and rivers each year. These toxins can kill fish, crabs, birds, and other wildlife and get into the water we drink. Other toxins leak from landfills, hazardous waste dumps, and mining operations near streams. Airborne pollutants, which combine with rain and fall as acid rain, can be deadly to stream insects, plants, and fish. Thermal pollution is also a danger. Many industrial plants release warm water that can doom cold-water species such as trout. But other types of fish, often nonnative, may thrive under these conditions.

Runoff   Rain and melting snow wash pollutants off the land and into streams and rivers. This pollution is called runoff. Runoff comes from many sources, including pesticides and herbicides. These chemicals, which are used to kill crop pests and weeds, wash off farmland, lawns, and golf courses. They run off into rivers and streams, where the chemicals can weaken or kill aquatic organisms. Fertilizers used on farms and lawns can be damaging, too. Like sewage and manure, fertilizers increase bacterial growth, which uses up the stream's oxygen, causing aquatic animals to suffocate.

More Runoff   Those slick, rainbow-colored patches of oil and gas on pavement can wash into rivers and streams. When rainwater flows over pavement, it picks up pollutants from leaking car oil, gas, construction debris, garbage, car wash soap, and other chemicals along the way. (It only takes 1 quart [about 1 liter] of motor oil to pollute 2 million gallons [7.6 million liters] of water.) Oil and gas get into streams not only from cars but also from boat engines and leaking underground storage tanks.

Muddy Problems   Removing trees and plants from streamsides increases erosion. Strong rains wash soil that was once held by plant roots into streams and rivers. These particles can clog fish's gills, causing suffocation, as well as blocking sunlight that aquatic plants need. Road building and construction greatly accelerate erosion. Some states have laws that require developers to erect silt barriers made of fabric, plastic, or straw bales to prevent sediment from washing into streams.

STENCILING STORM DRAINS

Many products we use at home and in the yard—cleansers, paints, nail polishes, mothballs, pesticides, and motor oils—contain toxic ingredients. When these chemicals are dumped on driveways, in streets, and down storm drains, they can flow directly into streams, rivers, and estuaries, polluting them.

Educate your community about this pollution problem by stenciling warnings on storm drains to let people know where their waste ends up. Student groups all over the country are carrying out these projects. Some groups stencil words, such as "This Way to Ocean" or "Drains to Bay" or "Warning: This Drain Leads to a Stream." Others stencil pictures, like a picture of a fish saying, "Our Habitat Is Down the Drain." More commonly, they stencil a simple fish symbol and educate the local community so that people will know what that symbol means and why it is important.

Stenciling storm drains can raise community awareness about water pollution.

Materials you will need:

- Cardboard (cereal boxes work well)
- Scissors or an X-Acto knife (use only with adult supervision)
- Nontoxic blue latex paint
- Paint stirrers
- Paintbrushes and/or paint sponges
- Old rags and water for cleaning brushes

Before you begin making stencils, lay the groundwork for your campaign. Get together with other people who may want to help you. Decide which drains you want to stencil. Contact your town council and get their approval before carrying out your project. Then set a stenciling day. At this time, you may also want to contact the local newspaper, television station, and radio stations in case they want to cover your project. This will help you get the word out about the stencils. Then you can get down to the basics:

1. Make stencils ahead of time, by cutting out the desired pattern in the cardboard.
2. At the storm drain site, place the stencil on the pavement in front of the drain.
3. Have someone hold the stencil in place while another person brushes on the paint.
4. Remove the stencil. Correct any mistakes with a brush or sponge.
5. Repeat the stenciling on the pavement at the top of the drain.
6. Clean brushes or sponges with water when done.
7. Follow up on your project by educating the public about the pollution problem and what the stencils mean. Then pat yourself on the back for a job well done!

For more information on drain stenciling programs, contact:
Clean Ocean Action
P.O. Box 505
Highlands, NJ 07732
Phone 1-908-872-0111

OTHER THREATS

At least twenty-one million people in Mexico and in Colorado, New Mexico, Wyoming, Utah, Nevada, California, and Arizona rely on the Colorado River system's water to grow food, water lawns, raise fish, produce electricity, water cattle, float boats, run industry, fill swimming pools, and supply drinking water fountains. Just one golf course may use 1.5 million gallons (5.7 million liters) of water in a day! When water is drawn from rivers for people's use, aquatic animals and plants suffer from reduced water levels.

Exotic Species   For decades, people have been introducing exotic, or nonnative, fish, snails, mussels, crayfish, plants, and other organisms into North American streams. Some of these introductions occurred when the organisms hitched rides in boat ballast, were dumped from bait buckets, or were released from aquariums by pet owners. But other introductions were carried out by fishery managers on purpose, in order to satisfy fishermen's demand for sport and commercial fish of particular species. The results of these introductions can be disastrous. Exotic fish often outcompete native fish, eating their eggs and young fish and pushing them out of nesting sites. Competition with exotic species is one of the leading causes of fish extinction in North America.

A RIVER SUCCESS STORY

Twenty-five years ago, the Connecticut River stank. The river smelled so bad and had so much raw sewage and trash floating in it that few people desired to live on its banks. In places, the river ran different colors on different days, depending on what dye the factories were using. Yet today, the river is cleaner, odorless, beautiful—a magnet for recreational fishermen, boaters, birds, and bird-watchers.

Great Successes   What changed? The law. The 1972 Clean Water Act funded and improved wastewater treatment

· THE TEN MOST ENDANGERED RIVERS ·
IN THE UNITED STATES

Each year, a conservation group called American Rivers evaluates the threats to rivers in the United States and issues a list of the most endangered and threatened ones.

Here are the ten most endangered rivers for 1995:

1. Clarks Fork of the Yellowstone River (Montana, Wyoming)
Threat: proposed gold mine

2. Los Angeles River (California)
Threats: flood-control project, urban neglect

3. Columbia and Snake Rivers (Washington, Oregon, Idaho)
Threats: dam project, water scarcity because of water use for irrigation

4. Animas River (Colorado)
Threat: water development projects that confine the river in channels and withdraw water for irrigation and drinking water

5. Missouri River (Midwest, Great Plains)
Threats: channelization for navigation and pollution from farm pesticides and fertilizers

6. Kansas River (Kansas)
Threats: dredging and pollution from farm pesticides and fertilizers

7. Mississippi River (Midwest)
Threats: flood-control projects and pollution from farm pesticides and fertilizers

8. Cheat River (West Virginia)
Threats: proposed dam, pollution from mining

9. Penobscot River (Maine)
Threat: proposed dam

10. Thorne River (Alaska)
Threat: habitat destruction from timber harvesting

Source: American Rivers, 1995

A group prepares to explore the Connecticut River by canoe.

plants. The Connecticut River began recovering. Citizens pitched in and helped. Now, although the river is not perfectly clean, much of it is fishable. The river's story illustrates problems but successes, too, and most of all, what can be done by people who are willing to work hard to reverse previous ecological damage and to prevent it from continuing in the future.

New Challenges   Today, the Connecticut River is facing new threats. It's such a scenic river, so close to major cities, that it attracts people who want to boat it, fish it, and build houses on its banks. Unfortunately, overuse of this kind could ultimately hurt the river as well. However, steps are being taken to protect the river. In 1991, the Silvio O. Conte National Fish and Wildlife Refuge was established to protect the river and its banks. Without borders and gates, the refuge is more of a plan than a place, a new kind of refuge sewn together from government-owned and private land.

Grants and incentives will encourage landowners to protect river habitat. In the long term, conserving the river will be a complex project involving many different people. But the future looks bright for the Connecticut.

MORE RIVER-SAVING EFFORTS

All over North America and the rest of the world, people are working together to clean up and protect rivers, and to use them more wisely. Many of the leaders of these efforts are kids and young adults. Here are just a few of the recent efforts being made on behalf of rivers:

- In June 1993, the government of British Columbia designated a new wilderness park called Tatshenshini-Alsek. Establishing the park halted plans for open-pit copper mines that would have polluted the Tatshenshini River, a wild river popular with white-water rafters.
- Students in Detroit, Michigan, carried out a petition drive to stop the building of a golf course that would have degraded a local creek.
- In South Bend, Indiana, local volunteers periodically gather to clear trash from the banks of the Saint Joseph River.
- Through Project Del Rio, 4,000 high-school students from Texas and Mexico have participated in a program that includes analyzing the pollution content of water from the Rio Grande.
- In Washington, state funds are being used to hire unemployed timberworkers to restore salmon habitat by improving the conditions of creek banks and rivers.
- In California, volunteers for The Nature Conservancy planted cottonwoods, willows, and oaks to restore the riparian habitat along the Kern River, an important nesting site for the western race of the yellow-billed cuckoo.

- While monitoring a stream, high-school students in Farmington, Michigan, discovered a malfunctioning sewage valve. The situation was reported to government officials, who then repaired the valve.
- Through a global network called GREEN (Global Rivers Environmental Education Network), elementary, middle-school, and high-school students in North America, Asia, Latin America, Africa, and Europe are testing for water pollution and exchanging information by letter and computer about their local rivers and their conservation problems and solutions.

From Alabama to Africa, from Canada to China, people who care about rivers are working to save them. Their efforts not only help save wildlife habitat but also protect the places where people swim, the fish they eat, and the water they drink. Rivers, among the most polluted of aquatic biomes, will need the help of many people to recover from past pollution and remain clean and free-flowing in the future. For tips on how you can get involved in conserving rivers and streams, read the next section.

RESOURCES AND WHAT
YOU CAN DO TO HELP

Here's what you can do to help ensure that rivers and streams are conserved:

• Learn more by reading books and watching videos and television programs about rivers and streams. Check your local library, bookstore, and video store for resources. Here are just a few of the books available for further reading:

Adopting a Stream: A Northwest Handbook by Steve Yates
(University of Washington Press, 1989).
Fish: An Enthusiast's Guide by Peter B. Moyle (University of
California Press, 1993).
Fish Watching: An Outdoor Guide to Freshwater Fishes by C.
Lavett Smith (Comstock, 1994).
Floods by Brian Knapp (Raintree-Steck Vaughn, 1990).
Hudson River, An Adventure From the Mountains to the Sea by
Peter Lourie (Boyds Mills Press, 1992).
Pond and River by Steve Parker (Knopf Books for Young
Readers, 1988).
Yukon River, An Adventure to the Gold Fields of the Klondike by
Peter Lourie (Boyds Mills Press, 1992).

• For more information on conservation issues related to rivers and streams, contact the following organizations:

American Rivers
801 Pennsylvania Avenue SE
Suite 400
Washington, DC 20003
Phone 1-202-547-6900
E-mail: amrivers@igc.apc.org

River Network
P. O. Box 8787
Portland, OR 97207-8787
Phone 1-503-241-3506

Chesapeake Bay Foundation
162 Prince George Street
Annapolis, MD 21401-9983
Phone 1-410-268-8816

If you like the job these organizations are doing, consider becoming a member.

• Get your class, ecology club, 4-H Club, Girl Scout troop, Boy Scout troop, or other organization involved in monitoring and preventing pollution in a stream or river near you. Have your teacher, leader, or adviser contact one of the following organizations for information:

Global Rivers Environmental Education Network (GREEN)
721 East Huron Street
Ann Arbor, MI 48104
Phone 1-313-761-8142
Internet: green@green.org
(They teach river monitoring and also sponsor computer conferences linking teachers, students, and citizens working on river issues worldwide.)

National Project Wet
Culbertson Hall
Montana State University

Bozeman, MT 59717

Phone 1-406-994-5392

(This organization publishes a variety of water-related educational guides and can connect educators with Project Wet activities and coordinators in their state.)

Save Our Streams Program

Izaak Walton League of America

707 Conservation Lane

Gaithersburg, MD 20878-2983

Phone 1-301-548-0150

(They teach river monitoring to classes. They also offer a free brochure on river pollution and what kids can do to help. To obtain this free brochure, call 1-800-BUG-4952.)

- Turn off lights, televisions, and other appliances when you are not using them. Saving electricity can prevent the need for coal mining and hydroelectric dams, which damage rivers and streams. Encourage your family to use energy-saving devices in your home. For more energy-saving tips, contact your local electric utility. For a catalog of energy-saving appliances and other environmental products, contact:

Real Goods

966 Mazzoni Street

Ukiah, CA 95482-3471

Phone 1-800-762-7325

Seventh Generation

Colchester, VT 05446-1672

Phone 1-800-456-1177

- Find out where your water comes from. Then work to reduce your water use. The less water you use, the more water there is available for aquatic animals and plants. Try taking shorter, more efficient showers and use less water when you brush your teeth. Your family might be able to install more efficient showerheads, faucets, and low-flow toilets. Reduce the amount of water used on lawns by watering in the evening, when less water evaporates. Better yet, replace lawns with other kinds of plants that are native to your area and don't require as much water. For information on water-saving devices, see the catalogs above.

• Reduce your use of toxic household substances, which can eventually end up in rivers and streams. For alternatives to commercially produced toxic products, see the catalogs above. For a catalog of less toxic household paints, wood finishes, and leather polishes, contact:

Livos Plant Chemistry
2641 Cerrilos Road
Santa Fe, NM 87501
Phone 1-505-988-9111

• Do not dump pet fish into streams or rivers. These animals are exotics—nonnatives. They do not belong in the wild. If they survive, they may compete with native fish or otherwise disrupt the natural ecosystem.

• Educate others about rivers and streams. Put on a skit at school or construct a display for the hallway or a local mall to raise awareness of river issues.

• Write letters to state and national government officials, telling them you feel river and stream conservation is important.

GLOSSARY

anadromous an organism that swims from the ocean up into the rivers to spawn

animal diversity the number of different species of animals

aquifer a porous layer of rock that can hold water within it

biome an area that has a certain kind of community of plants and animals

catadromous an organism that swims from rivers out into the ocean to spawn

delta a wide layer of silt deposited by a river where it flows into the ocean

detritus pieces of waste material—dead plants, dead animals, animal droppings, and so on—and the microorganisms that live on this material

drift the phenomenon of aquatic insects drifting downstream each evening

ecotone a border between two biomes, where the plants and animals of those biomes mingle

estuary a place where a river meets the ocean and salt water and fresh water mix

floodplain   the area a river covers with water when it spreads out during a flood

food web   a diagram that shows energy flow in a community by showing how the food chains in that community are linked

groundwater   water that is underground in spaces between particles of rock

headwater   the portion of a stream or river that is closest to its source

hydrologic cycle   the global circulation of water through lakes, streams, rivers, groundwater, the ocean, and atmosphere

levee   a wall of sediment that borders a stream or river channel and slopes away from the water. A levee may form naturally or be built by people to keep water out of a floodplain.

riffles   shallow, turbulent portions of a stream or river

riparian habitat   the habitat found on stream banks and riverbanks, where semiaquatic and terrestrial organisms mingle

river mouth   the place where a river ends by flowing into another body of water, such as a lake, the ocean, or another river

runoff   water that runs off the land and into streams, rivers, or lakes

sediment   particles of material that are transported and deposited by water, wind, or ice

spawning   the laying and fertilizing of eggs, by fish or amphibians

thermal pollution a human-caused change in water temperature that results in damage to aquatic life

tributary a stream or river that flows into another stream or river and contributes water to it

watershed the total area of land drained by a river or stream

water table the upper level that groundwater reaches in an aquifer

INDEX

river. *See also individual names of rivers.*
   banks, 18, 20, 27, 35, 41, 43, 44, 53, 58, 67
   boundary layer of, 29
   color of, 20
   endangered, 66
   headwaters, 19, 25
   mouth, 20, 24, 25, 27, 46
Rocky Mountains, 11, *12*, 13, *22*
rotifers, 30
runoff, 62

Sacramento River, *12*, 17
Saint Joseph River, 68
Saint Lawrence River, 11, *12*, 13
salamanders, 38, 39
salmon, 36, 38, 41, 52, *59*, 60, 68
Salmon River, 14
saltwater, 9, 27, 46, 47
sandbars, 21, 27, 45
sandhill cranes, 14, *15*
San Francisco Bay, 17
San Joaquin River, *12*, 17
sea cucumbers, 49, *49*
seas, 7, 15, 18, 20, 45, 47, 52
sediment, 9, 21, 22, 24, 27, 57, 60, 62
sewage, 53, 56, 60, 61, 62, 69
Sierra Madre, *12*, 13
silt, 20, *25*, 27, 47
snails, 29, 30, 31, 34, 48, 51
Snake River, *12*, 13
snow, 18, 19, 24, 62
spawning season, 36
springs, 11, 19, 25
sticklebacks, 36, 37
stonefly larvae, 31

storm drains, 63, *63*, 64
streams, types of, 9, 21, *22*, 43
suckers, 37, 38
sunfish, 36, 38
Suwannee River, 16, 20

Tahquamenon Falls, *16*
tannin, 16, *16*
Tennessee River, 11, *12*, 15
tides, 9, 46, 47
torrent beetles, 31
torrent moss, 25
tributaries, 13, 25
trout, 25, 29, 31, 33, 34, 42, 62
turbidity, 28
turtles, 8, 35, 38, 39, 44

valleys, 24, 25

water
   chemistry of, 28, 29
   drinking, 55, 56, 65, 69
   oxygen content of, 28, 29, 59
   temperature of, 28, 29, 59
   velocity of, 28, 29, 59
   volume of, 28, 29
water boatmen, 28, 33
waterfalls, 7, 22, 23, 27, 28, 43
water pennies, 31
watersheds, 11, *12*, 13
water striders, 28, 33, *33*
water table, 19
whirligig beetles, 3
worms, 10, 30, 31, 47, 48, 50, 51

Yangtze River, 7
Yukon River, 14

Zaire River, 7, 28

PHOTO CREDITS

p. 8: © C. C. Lockwood/Earth Scenes; p. 15: © Charlie Palek/ Animals Animals; p. 16: © Jeff Sayre; p. 22: Karen Tweedy/Earth Scenes; p. 23: © Ralph A. Reinhold/Earth Scenes; p. 25: NASA/ TSADO/Tom Stack & Associates; p. 30 (left): Peter Parks/Oxford Scientific Films/Animals Animals; p. 30 (right): Oxford Scientific Films/Animals Animals; p. 33: © Hermann Eisenbeiss/Photo Researchers, Inc.; p. 39: Z. Leszczynski/© Animals Animals; p. 40: © Eric Gravé/Photo Researchers, Inc.; p. 42: © Peter Weimann/ Animals Animals; p. 46: © Jeff Foott/Tom Stack & Associates; p. 49 (top): © Bruce Watkins/Animals Animals; p. 49 (bottom): B. G. Murray Jr./Animals Animals; p. 52: © Pat & Tom Leeson/ Photo Researchers, Inc.; p. 56: Reuters/Bettmann; p. 59: © John Shaw/ Tom Stack & Associates; p. 63: © Greg Vaughn/Tom Stack & Associates; p. 67: © Ted Levin/Earth Scenes.